A MORNING CUP WITH HONEY

Lady Tonya Dixson

KILGORE PUBLISHING
Flint Michigan
Since 2015

A Morning Cup with Honey
Copyright © Lady Tonya Dixson 2017
Kilgore Publishing

All rights are reserved. Except as permitted under the U.S. Copyright Act of 1976, no part of the publication may be reproduced, distributed or transmitted in any form or by any means, or stored in a database or retrieval system without the prior written permission of the publisher.

All scriptures used in this book are taken from the New Living Translation version of the Holy Bible, Copyright © 1996, 2001 and 2003. All rights reserved.

For more information about this book, speaking engagements or ordering in volume (qualifying organizations) please email ladytd.sis@gmail.com.

ISBN 978-0-9961347-5-0
For Worldwide Distribution
Printed in the U.S.A.

2 Thessalonians 2:16-17

₁₆ May our Lord Jesus Christ himself and God our Father, who loved us and by his grace gave us eternal encouragement and good hope, ₁₇ encourage your hearts and strengthen you in every good deed and word.

Table Contents

Dedication

Foreword by Pastor Kevin Dixson

A Personal Word

An Important Message

Acknowledgements

A Tiny Spark...1

Not Being Impatient While Waiting 3

New Way of Thinking 5

For Real, For Real SAVED 7

Trust & Believe 9

Smiling ~At-Cha~ 10

We Are Winners 12

Something about God's Grace 14

Dismiss It and Keep It Mov'in.........................16

Transparency Concerning my Honey................18

Spiritual Debt 22

Invisible Evidence 24

Hard Head Makes a Soft Behind 25

Renew Me Oh God! 29

Choose Wisely 31

New Day to Thrive 33

A Conversation with My Girls........................35

This Recipe Doesn't take Generic Ingredients..................37
Design Your Own Happiness ……………………..39
Peacefully Rest in Chaos …………………………....41
Don't Let Your Struggles Block Your Blessings ………43
Unique By-Right …………………………………..45
10 of My Favs …………………………...................47
You Don't Know …………………………………49
Family Gives Strength…………………………….....51
Quench This Thirsting …………………………….53
Praise to God …………..……………………………55
He Listens ………………………………………….....57
Obligation to Work ………………………………….59
Do-Over Please! ……………………………….…...61
Pure Foolishness ……………………………………...63
Lady Tonya Dixson ……………………………….64

DEDICATION

I dedicate this book to the Holy Spirit whom - I believe - has been teaching me to be an encourager, to everyone I meet, daily.

The purpose of this book is to encourage you to spend a moment with the Lord and have *"A Morning Cup* with me before you start your day.

This book is not intended to be a replacement for reading God's word - the Bible; nor is it meant to keep you from having your personal time with the Lord.

I encourage you to utilize this book in combination with your daily devotional time.

Enjoy this day,
Lady Tonya Dixson

FOREWARD

It's morning, and your eyes have opened, looking forward to another day full of God's grace and opportunities. You think *"because I see another day, GOD'S agenda through me is not done yet."*
As your mind gets warmed up for the responsibilities headed your way you sit down and have a cup of your favorite morning jolt.

Some people may have coffee or tea to get them going, but the effects will soon wear off. Having a morning cup with Lady Tonya will not only bless your mind with spiritual caffeine, but it will change your heart.

People are hurting and confused wanting to be loved, but at the same time, they don't know how to give it. What will make this book an extraordinary journey for you is that GOD has anointed Lady Tonya with words of power; to overcome any life situation. It's refreshing to have *A Morning Cup with Honey* any time of the day.

Love You Always,
Your husband
Kevin

A Personal Word

Honey - I love you so much. You are a true ministry of what the power of God can do in the lives of those who obey. You have taught me the importance of character and integrity because of who you are in the light.

Thank you for your display of character; I am privileged to be your wife. For all your attention, diligence, time and especially for reminding me of just who I am in Christ, I am genuinely grateful. I pray that our three young men will be the confidants, encouragers, friends, husbands, teachers, and great men based on what they've witnessed as they grew in our home.

Keith, Kalen, and Keinyi – you all are the apples of mom's eye and the beat to mom's heart!

When you were born, I prayed that the Lord would keep you in perfect peace; that he would wrap His loving arms around you, shield you, protect you, shape you, mold you and make you. Since that time, I have prayed for you, regularly. I pray as you find your way in this life you will lay aside any sin and hindrance, which will so easily entangle you. I pray you will run the race set before you with endurance. You are handsome and blessed beyond measure. Never settle! Never forget who you are or whose you are.

 My sister Zaire - I can't imagine life without you. When you were born, and I felt your warm touch I knew our bond would never be broken. Since that time, I have prayed continuously for you. You are a beautiful young lady, and God has blessed you beyond imagination. Never forget how precious you are to me and in His sight.

I love you,
Sissy

A morning cup…..with Honey, wisdom, and truth,
Stir it up…..
This cup is just for you…..
Start your day with no commotion!
A morning cup with scripture & devotion…..
Written just for you Sissy,
Love you always
~Your Sister~
Zaire N. Jackson

An Important Message

If you have never met Jesus Christ, you can know him today. God cares so much for you and wants to help you in every area of your life. That is why He sent Jesus to die for you. You can make your life right with God this very moment and make Heaven your home. Would you pray this prayer with me?

Oh God, I ask you to forgive me of my sins. I believe you sent Jesus to die on the cross for me. I receive Jesus Christ as my personal Lord and Savior. I confess Him as Lord of my life, and I give my life to Him.

Thank you, Lord, for saving me and for making me new. In Jesus name, Amen.

If you prayed this prayer, I would welcome you to the family of God. Please let me know about your decision for Jesus by emailing me at ladytd.sis@gmail.com. I want to send you some free literature to help you and your new walk with the Lord. I am so SUPER EXCITED for you!

Acknowledgments

With special thanks:

♥ To my daughter-in- Love Jennifer thank you for allowing me to be in your life and for bringing our two beautiful babies Kayleigh and Korey into the world. You are truly what our family has been missing all these years, and we didn't know it until you came to be with us.

♥ To my Sisters, prayer partners and fellow praying wives, Aysha Boykins and Nicole Dixson- Mays who have experienced, along with me, what gut-level, crying out to God and what intercession for a husband really means. Without your deep, faithful commitment to God and prayer, this book might never have been written. You two are Eternal Treasures in my heart.

♥ To Sisters in Season (S.I.S) community and women's ministry. Thank you for your love and support. I have come to realize any time you do something for God by helping, inspiring and encouraging others- He notices the sincerity of your heart and acts of kindness which will not go on rewarded by Him. I desire to encourage, motivate and you to help someone by merely sharing A Morning Cup with Honey.

♥ To Sis. Precious Brown Power N You, Love Power, and Purpose. Your obedience to God with these two platforms has inspired me to pull this book off the shelf, adopt accountability and bring it to life once again. I thank you for your encouragement, and a triple thank you for your expertise and putting up with me during this project. You are a delight.

♥ To my Pastor the late H.B Dixson and Pastor Kevin Dixson for teaching me how to pray, encouraging me and teaching me to ALWAYS be led by the Holy Spirit.

A Morning Cup with Honey

A Tiny Spark

I can remember ever so clearly our boys playing sports from their youth all the way through college. I was the one praying and of course their biggest cheerleader. Now, Honey, on the other hand, was right there along the fence line during football season and on the very first bleacher at all the basketball games YELLING! I often had to separate myself from him because I thought he was being mean, too harsh and sometimes embarrassing.

After many rides home listening to the boys and the interaction between them and their dad, the gleam in their eyes and the excitement in their voices, I found that to be far from my truth. It's just merely their way of communicating. The boys would be discussing the highlights in the back of the van. I'd hear them say "I heard dad when he told me to cut to the outside", or when dad yelled "GET YOUR HEAD UP AND STOP DRIBBLING WITH YOUR HEAD DOWN", or when one brother would say to the other "that was tight when you passed the ball to.....", and the other brother would respond "I heard dad say he was open, he told me to do that." I could never understand how the boys could hear their dad's voice over the chants, the cheers, and roaring crowds. They'd even make eye contact with Honey as a form of communication at times during the game.

Understand, GOD is not interested in the cheers and the roaring crowd because that doesn't guarantee victory. What He is concerned about is you hearing Him and knowing His voice through the crowd to receive His instructions. It's there where you are guaranteed victory.

What a powerful tool each of us is blessed with communication! Depending on its delivery and timing, something as simple as a point, laugh or cheer has the power to make a jovial youth radiate or cut them to their core. Use your tongue for God's purposes by building up loved ones, teaching others about Jesus' love, or praying in stressful situations.

James 3:5
In the same way, the tongue is a small thing that makes grand speeches. But a tiny spark can set a great forest on fire.

A Morning Cup with Honey

Not Being Impatient While Waiting

Years ago, my honey and I prayed for full-time Ministry after a process of deep frustration. The hunger and frustration were brought about through the realization that the church exists for a much bigger purpose than itself.

This began a transitioning process within from a "church-centered" or "religious-activity-centered" culture where the focus is upon us, to a more Kingdom-centered culture where our focus is on fulfilling God's agenda. It didn't come with a cute little bow or at a time that we thought it should. It happened unexpectantly.

Just because you can't see how God is going to do it, doesn't mean He isn't. Ahhhhh, THE GREAT I AM is known for His undeniable, and "unconventional moves." He wants everybody to know, including you, that HE is still the MIRACLE WORKING GOD that called you for His Purpose! He is Lord of Lords and King of Kings.

So, just tell them very politely, Keep Watching! God is ready to give them something to see. And it will be all for His Glory.

Lady Tonya Dixson

Romans 8:24-25
We were saved to have this hope. If we can see what we are waiting for, that is not really hope. People don't hope for something they already have. But we are hoping for something we don't have yet, and we are waiting for it patiently.

A Morning Cup with Honey

New Way of Thinking

For a week or so everything related to business and ministry has been moving slowly. Things hadn't been lining up the way the vision was given to me. I felt like everything had been moving at a snail's pace and not being accomplished. But guess what! The wheels of progress don't always move as fast as we would like.

Then one day I was driving to the Salon, and in my quiet time, I purposefully shifted my mind not to focus on the speed of the wheels, just make sure that the wheels are moving in the right direction! Then a client came in with a similar situation, she had been having issues with her business and people not understanding what she was trying to accomplish. Imagine the look on my face due to my own situation.

The Lord had already prepared me for this conversation. I was able to explain to her that capacity is the maximum amount that something can contain. Capacity is the ability or power to do, experience, or understand something. Don't get frustrated with all those who can't grasp your vision, maybe they just don't have the capacity. Stop trying to share your 50-million-dollar vision with someone who has a $0.50 capacity! When your vision manifests, it changes your circle. Continue to speak His truths. People may not like it, but that is okay.

LORD make my mouth a fountain of life, to encourage, speak kind, tenderhearted affectionate words to people. Let my mouth be full of life. No matter how I feel.

Ezekiel 36:26
I will put a new spirit in you to change your way of thinking. I will take out the heart of stone from your body and give you a tender, human heart.

A Morning Cup with Honey

For Real, For Real SAVED

I tell you the truth! When I came into the knowledge and knew that I was saved for real, for real. Not my momma and grandma telling me I was saved but on my own merit and through my individual situations with prayer and supplication. My finding the truth in the midst of my sin and Him consuming me from the inside out. WHEW GOD!

Holiness and freedom from sin are not obtained by struggling but by creating an environment within you that allows the Holy Spirit to transform you from within. If you sow into your spirit instead of your flesh, you will create an atmosphere of spiritual growth. That new life within your spirit will be released to begin the process of transforming your soul. Your flesh and your spirit will always be in a battle, but you have the choice of which one will be in control.

The thoughts you allow to stay in your mind will determine whether you control your flesh, or whether your flesh controls you. Your whole life will be transformed, from the inside out, as you allow the Holy Spirit to change you through prayer and God's Word. You may not even notice the transformation taking place, but one day you will look back and realize you are no longer a caterpillar, but a beautiful butterfly, floating above the reach of sin, living your life in the beauty of holiness.

Romans 12:1-2

So, I beg you, brothers and sisters, because of the great mercy God has shown us, offer your lives as a living sacrifice to him—an offering that is only for God and pleasing to him. Considering what he has done, it is only right that you should worship him in this way. Don't change yourselves to be like the people of this world, but let God change you inside with a new way of thinking. Then you will be able to understand and accept what God wants for you. You will be able to know what is good and pleasing to him and what is perfect.

A Morning Cup with Honey

Trust and Believe

Can't nobody tell Honey and me nothing about our Keith, Kalen, and Keinyi! Point Blank Period. Isn't that how it is? Parents see their own children differently than other people do?

As believers in Jesus, it's the same way with our heavenly Father. You are the apple of His eye. No matter what, He sees you as His most perfect creation. He is proud of you. You are the joy of His heart. You may make some mistakes; you may fall; you may make a mess, but He is right there ready to pick you up, dust you off and calm your soul. In His eyes, you are an overcomer; you are victorious; you are strong. In His eyes, you are pure and whole. He's our protector and defender. No man can not hinder us.

Today, I encourage you to trust in His love, trust in His goodness, and trust that you can find safety and rest in Him.

Deuteronomy 33:27
God lives forever. He is your place of safety.
His power continues forever! He is protecting you.
He will force your enemies to leave your land. He will say,
'Destroy the enemy!'

Lady Tonya Dixson

~Smiling Atcha~

I have a facebook page, and I end each morning post by saying…

"Let's make it A GREAT DAY!

~ Smiling Atcha~"

This just means that we can dictate our day. We can speak to our day and declare that it's going to be good and then live it out with our actions by making a choice to have a good day, all while smiling because, at the end of the day, God did that thing!

Today I encourage you not to let the negative voices of the world steal your focus or get you off course. Don't start planning for a bad day. Choose to prepare for good. The scripture doesn't say, "Plan for good as long as your car is running well." It doesn't say, "Plan for good as long as your marriage is strong." It doesn't say, "Plan for good as long as you aren't facing any adversity."

No, we can plan for good because we serve a God who is good, and He is ready, willing and able to bring us through any adversity we face! Boldly plan for good today and watch God show up in the midst of your plans!

A Morning Cup with Honey

2 Corinthians 4:13
The Scriptures say, "I believed, so I spoke." Our faith is like that too. We believe, and so we speak.

Now let's make it A GREAT DAY!
~ Smiling Atcha~

We Are Winners

I had to sit and go through my own personal counseling session with my Honey (*which I do quite often, one of the benefits of him being my Pastor* ☺). I was perplexed as to why women find it so hard to sincerely support one another, making it uncomfortable and hard to be one's self.

Could it be that some are insecure in their own right, some may just be in a dark place, selfish or intimidated by other women; their goals or accomplishments, to say the least. The conversation was very much needed and ended with "we as Women need to exercise how we can avoid falling into the trap of comparison and competing with each other and find the ultimate contentment in Christ."

When God is stretching us, or requiring growth from us, He has a way of making us very uncomfortable. Do not change, don't jump ship, don't compare your beginning to someone else's middle, simply stay the course, **your** course. It may hurt, it may get lonely but be true, be who God ordained you to be. Do not dim your light to appease darkness, but Shine **your** light to reprove the darkness.

A Morning Cup with Honey

Many times, you will be misunderstood, but the God who holds **ALL POWER** will stand with you during the persecution. Great will be your reward. Love. Forgive. Heal. When people are intimidated by you, just because of who you are, you must know that it's their issue, not yours. Pray for them, but don't stop being you.

Choose to be light and **love**, anyway. YOU ARE A WINNER AND THE FIGHT YOU'RE IN PROVES IT! Speak what God says! BE WHO GOD ORDAINED! And let Him vindicate you.

Matthew 5:11-12

"People will insult you and hurt you. They will lie and say all kinds of evil things about you because you follow me. But when they do that, know that great blessings belong to you. Be happy about it. Be very glad because you have a great reward waiting for you in heaven. People did these same bad things to the prophets who lived before you.

REMEMBER: YOU ARE CHOSEN BY GOD. ITS JUST PART OF THE PROCESS. 🖤🖤🖤

Lady Tonya Dixson

Something about God's Grace

My eyes popped open. As I stare into the darkness, all I can do is lift my hands and say *"Thank you Lord for waking me to see another day. What is your plan for me this day, what would you have me to do, who would you have me to serve, who would you have me to stay away from today!"*

Our baby boy is out the door headed for work, my honey is sleeping next to me. In minutes, his alarm will go off, and the demands of the day will rush us like a shopping mall during the holidays; super busy with a crowd of meetings, counseling sessions, visits, Bible studies, clients, rehearsals, and deadlines. For the millionth time, I'll make breakfast, check schedules, and organize the day but through it all, I still cannot make sense of this thing called LIFE.

Are you with me this morning? Does this sound like you? Sounds like a mess, doesn't it? But God is so amazing! You see, the devil wants to cloud your mind with doubt. His strategy is to get your eyes off what God said and on the circumstances of life. Don't let him play games in your mind. Refuse to let his schemes paralyze you with fear to such a degree that you forget that you've got power.

Show the devil that you won't stand for his criminal attacks on your life anymore.

Through all the hustle and bustle I encourage you to just **STOP**, take a breath and listen to His calming voice He answers every question. He answers our questions with one word: GRACE! His grace is sufficient, and it calls us to change. His grace gives us the power to pull it all off! Hallelujah!!!

Hebrews 4:16
With Jesus as our high priest, we can feel free to come before God's throne where there is grace. There we receive mercy and kindness to help us when we need it.

Lady Tonya Dixson

Dismiss It and Keep It Mov'in

Forgive and keep it mov'in! God is moving too strategically in your life. You have no time to entertain foolishness. Dismiss it. And get back to the grind.

Yes, I admit it! I had become overwhelmed, defeated, down in the dumps, extremely hard on myself and no way to dress it up and make it look pretty. I wasn't in a good place because of naysayers. One day the Lord ministered to me and told me I would be healed from the wounds of others. Wow!

It took me a long time to understand exactly what that meant, but eventually, I got it. I can't blame naysayers, I must trust God and keep it mov'in while believing just what He says. God has put seeds of greatness inside of me. I refuse to accept lack and defeat as my destiny. It may have been that way in the past, but God raised me up to set a new standard.

He's an *even now* God. I had to do my part and have *even now* faith. Through this, I found that we all have many wounds from this life. We will go through many trials, but as we help one another, to heal and sow our love into others, we will receive healing in return.

I have ministered and served many times amid my struggles and my own pain. I don't know how to do it any other way. Simply because of that old familiar scripture found in Hebrews 11:1 "Now faith is the substance of things hoped for, the evidence of things not seen."

When you give sincere love, you will receive more love in return, it may not come from the place you sowed it, but it will come back. That's just how Faith works.
I encourage you to sow without expectations. Sowing and reaping work in every situation, it must come back in return simply because God is not slack concerning His promises to us.

Galatians 6:7-9
"If you think you can fool God, you are only fooling yourselves. You will harvest what you plant. If you live to satisfy your sinful self, the harvest you will get from that will be eternal death. But if you live to please the Spirit, your harvest from the Spirit will be eternal life. We must not get tired of doing good. We will receive our harvest of eternal life at the right time. We must not give up."

Lady Tonya Dixson

Transparency Concerning My Honey

My Honey wears so many hats, yet he is a constant to his family, and I'm guilty of expecting him to always be. He has been a very stable person in my life. He is a laid-back, humble very even-tempered kind of man. He is patient, logical, strong, and full of faith. He leans on God. Knowing who he is and what he has shown me about his character, helps me quickly realize moments when he is not okay.

When he is impatient, not thinking clearly, or acting down, it raises awareness in me that he is not okay. When he expresses anything different than what I am familiar with, I get aggravated, as if what he is experiencing is a bother to me, an inconvenience, something I don't want to deal with.

There is a part of me that wonders why he is being so sensitive or responding so out of character. Anything that is not familiar seems hard to me. It takes me over, and I don't know what to do. Instead of putting a halt to my own agenda and what I am trying to do, I snap at him. I make comments that I want to be encouraging to him in hopes of helping him refocus or brush off what he is going through so that he can keep being my constant. But, by not explicitly addressing what I see, my words become a thorn in his side, a fresh cut to his heart. YES, I admit there have been moments I have been so frustrated with him not being okay.

Although I know not to raise my voice at my Husband, it takes everything in me not to do it. Sometimes I want to grab him and shake him, wake him up. I want to remind him of the man I know he is. In those moments, I don't realize I am being insensitive. However, after a few of my comments, he usually shoots one back such as, *"If you know I am having a hard day, why aren't you trying to help me?"*

I should simply affirm him. I don't know why it is hard for me when he is the one having a hard day. I have failed at this more times than not. I think I let my flesh rule during those moments.

I can be a very selfish person as related to my Honey. I can also be sensitive and emotional. I am the one who is unstable and has hard days. So, why can't I let my Honey have days like that? I know what it feels like and I know extra love is needed on those days. So, why can't I be a wife who sees when her husband is not okay and steps into love more? I want to be, I truly do.

My husband can have hard days, and I want to be a wife who can help him through it.

It takes meditation in scripture, reminders of holiness and the value of meekness for me to remember to be mild and pleasant to him. Then I commit my heart to be a wife who knows her husband so well that my heart is sensitive to when he is sensitive. I commit to being a wife who is willing to let her husband's needs be above her own. I commit to being a wife who is not easily frustrated. I commit to being a wife who intentionally uses her words to build up her husband. I commit to being caring and loving and giving more on the days that require more.

If you have struggled with this; if somewhere in your heart you believe your husband is your constant, and anything outside of that is unacceptable if your husband is having a hard day and you are not helping by stepping in and loving him through it…I want to challenge you to commit to being a wife that has a heart of understanding. I want to challenge you to change.

Our men can be sensitive. They were designed like we were, with emotions and responses to life. Our men will have experiences that lead to pain, suffering, unclarity, distraction, frustration, sadness, anger, and even depression. As much as they are strong, there are days where their weakness will show. Let us not be insensitive to their hearts. May we step in and love more than we ever have and let those things, on our agenda, that we feel so strongly to accomplish, go to pursue intimacy in marriage.

The devil has schemes to cause divisions in every relationship. You see… NO, it is not easy. He did not say that it would be, but I'm determined to put on the armor of God each day and fight to be the best that I can be in my marital covenant. Even when our struggle and hurt seems to be with this other person, we must remember: we have an enemy, and it's not each other.

Ephesians 6:12
"For our struggle is not against flesh and blood, but against the rulers, against the authorities, against the powers of this dark world and against the spiritual forces of evil in the heavenly realms,"

Lady Tonya Dixson

Spiritual Debt

    Whether it was a mother, father, aunt, grandmother or whoever it could have been, somebody loved us enough to put the seed of GOD in our lives. A road map to heaven through Jesus Christ never changes. We are in Spiritual Debt to pay this information forward to today's generation. Intentional living and passing forward the baton of our faith will ensure that God's Goodness, Love, and Faithfulness continue throughout the generations.

    A member of our congregation recently shared with us that her father, who moved out of state, shares his faith with his grandchildren by giving them a personal Bible Study, via phone, on a weekly basis - that's intentional! Our Son and daughter-in-love reading a bedtime story and saying prayers with our grandchildren - is intentional! Every time that our granddaughter and I are together we sing of the goodness of Jesus - that's intentional!

    We cannot assume our children are understanding and receiving faith from us. We must exemplify it, speak it, sing it, pray it and live it!

Psalm 100:5

For the Lord is good and his love endures forever; his faithfulness continues through all generations.

Invisible Evidence

Faith is a natural outcome of knowing who God is, not a goal to be attained. I think back to our boys and how they were tossed continuously in the air by Honey; a good Dad. They didn't study the physics of it all or ask for their father's previous tossed-to-drop ratio. Their faith was in who was about to throw them into the unknown, an outcome of a lifetime relationship that says, "I can trust my Dad."

The evidence of faith that I have with GOD is the higher He holds me up to a new level, the more confidence I have at a higher level that I have not seen yet.

Hebrews 11:1
Faith is what makes real the things we hope for. It is proof of what we cannot see.

Hard Head Makes a Soft Behind

There is only one thing more painful than learning from experience – and that is *not* learning from experience. Life is a journey, not a destination. It is through that journey we are born, broken, changed and shaped.

Life is God's chosen classroom in which He teaches His children how to love and live out His truth. One of the first and most vital truths we need to learn in our walk with God is obedience.

Truth does not change. We must change in response to the truth. A learned truth is an applied truth, and when we apply truth, we are practicing obedience. When we don't learn from our wrong choices, we are doomed to make the same mistakes again, falling back into disobedience. It is like going around the same old mountain again and again.

My Honey and I were richly blessed with 3 handsome, very athletic boys, who were very active in sports growing up. We traveled all over with the boys and their sports from youth through college and even professional games. All three went to college on Sports Scholarships. We had to pack them up and drive them to schools out of state. We all would pile into the car with all the things needed to get them set up for their journey, so we'd thought. I would say that honey and I were somewhat procrastinators when it came to having them ready to leave. We'd wait until the very last minute to shop for the things needed for them. It seemed that we would have learned from our oldest, Keith. After getting him set up, we had to make several trips back to the store to pick up items that were forgotten.

A couple summers later, everyone was excited about the next brother, Kalen, going off to school – until we discovered that no one had written down or taking inventory of the exact things needed– and once again, wasting valuable time. I took matters in hand, as exhausted as I was on the long ride home I grabbed a piece of paper and wrote down specific staple items that were needed. A few years later it was our last son Keinyi's summer, we were halfway to the point of departure, and everything was in writing when we discovered that we had no idea what had happened to the list. Once again, we went around that same old mountain, wasting time yet another year. I looked at Honey and said, "We must be slow learners."

I often wonder if our Father ever looks at the way we live and wonders, "Why are they so slow to learn and practice my truth?"

To *learn* the ways of God, we must *know* the truth of God. Saturating our lives with Scripture is essential to finding and doing God's will. The Bible is the roadmap, the blueprint, and the ultimate plan for our journey.

To walk in obedience to God, we must not only have the right directions for today, but we must also go back and destroy those paths of yesterday that once led us in the wrong direction.

Eliminating wrong choices makes the right decisions much easier to handle. Some of those old paths are familiar and may be hard to uproot. A friendship may have to be ended. A behavior pattern may have to be changed. A habit may have to be eliminated.

But if it leads to sin, if it makes it easier to sin, or if it entices or tempts you to sin, run from it! Don't go around that same old mountain of wrong choices again. Learn the lesson and choose obedience.

Ole school meaning which means those who keep making the same bad decisions and getting punished for it. Hard Head is saying you're going to do it your way only and the consequences are getting a butt whopping for it repeatedly. I'm so glad GOD'S Grace and Mercy is still in effect because by me still having a hard Head, nothing that's not like Him can get inside my head and if it does my soft behind can rest in his Grace and Mercy.

Romans 6:14
Sin will not be your master because you are not under law. You now live under God's grace.

A Morning Cup with Honey

Renew Me Oh God

It's Sunday.... the morning isn't starting off so well. I know I'm the Pastor's wife, but if there's anyone that needs faith to believe...it's me! I need to get beyond the man and open my heart to what God is saying through his servant! Yes, he's just a man, but he's God's mouthpiece! This Sunday I was praying! "Speak Lord, the door to my heart is wide open. I hear your voice, come in!"
While sitting in the front Pew, I wanted to roll over onto the floor and shout "AMEN" when Pastor said "procrastination is one of my biggest culprits and hurdles. Time is one of the most valuable commodities that you possess.

Procrastinate means to defer action or put off until another time. Time once lost, can never be recaptured. Procrastination is simply the cemetery where all your unfulfilled dreams have been buried. It's time to resurrect those dead dreams!" I wanted to yell in the church at the most inopportune time "FRUSTRATION IS MINE!"
Yes, I am the Pastors Wife, show me some grace PLEASE!

Frustration can take the joy right out of a great day. I ask myself, why so annoyed, why so frustrated? Then I burst into laughter when I realize I've been doing things my way...on my own strength...with my own instruction manual and I only see things my way because I've taken my eyes off His Word. No wonder!!! (SMH) I know I need to throw that manual away expeditiously!!!

Frustration is a common emotional response to opposition. It is a perceived resistance to the fulfillment of one's own will. (Wikipedia)

My prayer is, "Lord, help me take my eyes off worthless, non-prosperous, self-fulfilling ways. Give me life through Your Word! Open my eyes to your promises and to your truth so that my life will be renewed with Your goodness!"

Psalm 119:37-40

Turn my eyes from worthless things, and give me life through your word. Reassure me of your promise, made to those who fear you. Help me abandon my shameful ways; for your regulations are good. I long to obey your commandments! Renew my life with your goodness.

A Morning Cup with Honey

Choose Wisely

Be careful not to become offended today. An offense is a TRAP the devil has baited to cause you to stumble and fall! God wants us to be overcomers in every area of our lives which includes every offense that comes our way. Don't allow yourself to focus on the distraction, it can become a trap that keeps you from doing what God has for you to do. Instead, I encourage you to pray about your situation; then stand in faith in the midst.

As a child of the Most High God, your steps are ordered by Him. He has a specific place of blessing prepared for you. When you live a life of obedience to the Word of God, He promises to supply every one of your needs. Just as God directed Elijah to his place of blessing, God is leading you too. He's aligning the right opportunities for you and causing the right people to come along your path to help you get ahead. He's continually working behind the scenes on your behalf. But you must do your part to keep your heart open by following His Word and maintaining an attitude of faith and expectancy. A major key to keeping your heart in the right place is choosing peace and unity. The Bible says that when we live in unity, there He has commanded the blessing. And when your heart is in the place of blessing, the rest of your life will be in the place of blessing, too. Today, choose to be an overcomer, choose peace, choose obedience and choose the place of blessing.

John 16:1
These things have I spoken unto you, that ye should not be made to stumble.

A Morning Cup with Honey

New Day to Thrive

Good news, It's a New Day! Shake off all those negative thoughts of yesterday. Aren't you glad that His mercies are new every single morning! Choose to be happy today it's your choice. The time has come to get clear about who you are and what you choose.

Happiness is not just a random feeling as other people can think, happiness is a choice. It's a decision that we must make every day. All throughout life, you're going to have plenty of opportunities to lose your joy. We all go through disappointments. We all have times when things don't go our way. It's easy to let circumstances make us sour and dejected until we end up just going through the motions of day to day living. But if you're going to live in victory, if you're going to thrive the way God intends, you've got to make the decision that you're going to enjoy your life. You can choose to be happy despite your circumstances, every single day.

Today remember this is the day that the Lord has made for you to rejoice and be glad in it! As you choose joy, you are tapping into His strength which will carry you to victory all the days of your life.

There come moments in every person's life when a decision is necessary. A big decision. A major choice. Such a time is now. What you get to choose today is who you are and who you choose to be, and what you wish to experience in your life. Remember, not to decide is to decide.

I encourage you to spend some time with God in prayer this morning and begin again. Forget about ruffled feathers of yesterday and start fresh today.

Lamentations 3:23
Every morning he shows it in new ways! You are so very true and loyal!

A Morning Cup with Honey

A Conversation with My Girls

Let's get our feelings in check! God didn't choose me to have daughters. He's entrusted me with three boys and was raised with four brothers. So, you can say I'm straightforward, to the point and no holds barred when it comes to being emotional about certain things.

However, God did bless me with a boatload of beautiful nieces and one beautiful little sister, and I tell them all that there's so much more to life than finding someone who will want you or be sad over someone who doesn't. There's a lot of wonderful time to be spent discovering yourself without hoping someone will fall in love with you along the way, and it doesn't need to be painful or empty. You need to fill yourself up with love. Not anyone else. Become a whole being on your own. Go on adventures, sit in a coffee shop on your own, dress up for yourself, give to others, smile a lot. Live for yourself and be happy on your own. It isn't any less beautiful.

It is so amazing to be a child of the Most High God! YES!!! You may be going through the roughest storm of your life right now. You may be facing the toughest challenges. You may feel alone and abandoned by those closest to you.

There may be trouble all around you but in the very midst of your fear, your pain, and your loss. Jesus is there! HALLELUJAH!

He is your peace in the midst of the storm! He is your friend in the midst of loneliness! He is your comforter in the middle of your calamity! Draw near to Him, and He will draw near to you! He will surround you with songs of deliverance whenever you are afraid! He will rejoice over you with singing and dry all your tears! Weeping may endure for a night, but JOY comes in the morning! Joy is on its way to you, and it will arrive! His perfect peace is yours right now.

Philippians 4:7
And because you belong to Christ Jesus, God's peace will stand guard over all your thoughts and feelings. His peace can do this far better than our human minds.

A Morning Cup with Honey

This Recipe Doesn't Take Generic Ingredients

When my Honey wasn't a believer, I laid hands upon him every single night, begging God for his salvation. I know it wasn't up to me to save him. I prayed for years as I walked out the house with our children on our way to church weekly. I would see glimpses of the man that he could be for Christ, but still, he would turn down each request, we asked of him, to come with us to church, bible study, and youth meetings. He chose to go about his day his way. One night while praying, God gave me *Exodus 14:14 "You will not have to do anything but stay calm. The Lord will do the fighting for you."*

I look back to that season, and God taught me what it meant to be still and KNOW that He was God. I would like to encourage you to know that if you're praying about something and He doesn't answer you right away, He's working it out and it's something better than you could EVER imagine.

If you're struggling with your prayer life, know that the peace of Christ is within you. We are called to live within that peace. We are not to be anxious. Christ is in you; He is our hope! HALLELUJAH, my Honey did come to know the Lord, but not in my timing, not where and in the way in which I thought it would happen. God was cooking up something far better than I could have ever imagined; my way could have been a recipe for disaster. My objective was to Simply pray for my husband.

It was an example of the power of prayer. All the heartache, pain, and tears were exchanged for one moment of joy. One soul had been saved. And now when I look at my Honey, I see the fruit of the spirit. Love, joy, peace, patience, kindness all wrapped up in one man…Sent by God to be my earthly example of His mighty love.

Isaiah 55:8-9

The Lord says, "My thoughts are not like yours.
Your ways are not like mine.
Just as the heavens are higher than the earth,
so, my ways are higher than your ways,
and my thoughts are higher than your thoughts.

A Morning Cup with Honey

Design Your Own Happiness

Being a wife, mother, Pastors wife, NaNa, business owner and wearing many other hats, I don't get to choose what shakes my world, but I do get to decide what stabilizes it. I believe a lot of people give more out than they receive or at least give to themselves. Please remember there is a balance in life, in which anyone can operate by choice. I have learned in relationships, and that means business as well as family, to always give the best out and give the best to myself. Don't lose yourself so much in who you love until you're not living yourself. If I am treating others better than myself, what good am I?

This leads to burnouts, frustrations and quitting but if I treat myself well and others well then I can go the distance of success! Remember that God designed you. He knows exactly what makes you tick. He knows what makes you get out of bed in the morning, what makes you laugh, what makes you sit and cry in the wee hours of the morning. He knows what makes you feel motivated and what makes you feel like throwing in the towel. Nothing about you is a surprise to Him. But none of us are made perfectly. We are each flawed. And part of our time on earth is to become more of the person God created us to be.

So, STOP shining less so others can shine bright, shine bright so others can shine bright with you. Show yourself love first, so your cup can over follow to others. Ultimately giving to God first and He will take care of both you and them.

Luke 12:7
Yes, God even knows how many hairs you have on your head. Don't be afraid. You are worth much more than many birds.

A Morning Cup with Honey

Peacefully Rest in Chaos

The other night Honey and I went to see a movie. The movie was about a drilling rig exploding in the Gulf, igniting a massive fireball. Finding themselves fighting for survival as the heat and the flames become stifling and overwhelming. Banding together, the co-workers had to use their wits and listen to commands to make it out alive amid all the chaos.

It reminded me oh-so-well how the world around us gets so LOUD and drowns out the one still voice that needs to be heard. Chaos comes in all forms - family problems, financial problems, emotional stress or personal illness, just to name a few. Sometimes it seems like an onslaught of bad situations and other times it is little things that happen every now and then. Chaos is what we call it, but God calls it trials and testing.

It's hard to understand why, in the midst of chaos and even heart-ache, commands can delight us.
And he simply says, "Rest." Rest on my promises. Rest in my word. Rest in my purpose. Rest in my calling on your life. Rest in your faith. Rest in me. Rest in perfect peace it's the only peace that keeps us sane during the chaos. How do we obtain this perfect peace? By keeping our minds

steadfast, being focused on God and His word. By trusting in our Father, we are saying our plans and purposes is His plans and purpose.

Isaiah 26:3

God, you give true peace to people who depend on you, to those who trust in you.

A Morning Cup with Honey

Don't Let Your Struggles Block Your Blessings

Let's face it.... You're a BLESSING! My cousin is my Shero. She has no idea how much she blesses those in connection with her. I've watched her struggle with things throughout her life, and she always shows up for others, always manages to be a light in others path.

A few weeks ago, our car went down. It was going to cost us a couple grand to get it fixed. Lord, we are way too busy. What are we going to do? After we cried out to the Lord. Honey and I weren't worried we had an "OH WELL" attitude and was checking around doing some price comparison and different things. Meanwhile, the clock was still ticking we have no vehicle.

Suddenly, my cousin pulls up in the driveway and yells *"SOMEONE NEEDS TO TAKE ME HOME"* confused Honey took her home and we drove her car around for 2 weeks. The moral of this story is things may be a bit dark for you or just a little smoky but take courage in the fact that this is a new day!

You may be wondering if you will make it through and what awaits you if you do. As you move through, know this: You are someone's hero. A living example of faithful and cheerful perseverance.

Someone dares to meet the day simply because they see you do it. Someone sees GOD in you even when you feel you can't see God at all. On your worst day, you are a BLESSING. Isn't God amazing? And YES, that makes you amazing.

Let's get this day started. I would like to pray with you this morning: Father God give us the right thoughts, the right words, and the right actions to fulfill Your will for our lives. Grant us each the opportunity to be a blessing to someone in need. Let us be a channel of light in dark places, as well as, love, hope, and encouragement in this world. Erase our doubts and confusion; help us keep a pure heart, a peaceful spirit. And most of all, Thank You, God . . . for being our guide, our light, our keeper, our leaning post, and encourager. This is my prayer for us today. In Jesus name ~ Amen

Hebrews 13:16
And don't forget to do good and to share what you have with others because sacrifices like these are very pleasing to God.

A Morning Cup with Honey

Unique By-Right

I get asked all the time, "*How on earth can you juggle so much!?*" My answer – *"I can't, and I don't; It is all God, and that makes it all good."*

I can only do what I do because of Him. His surpassing power! Do I get exhausted, overwhelmed and sometimes feel like throwing in the towel? OF COURSE! But I take comfort in the intense words found in *2 Corinthians 4:7- We have this treasure from God, but we are only like clay jars that hold the treasure. This is to show that the amazing power we have is from God, not from us. 8: We have troubles all around us, but we are not defeated. We often don't know what to do, but we don't give up.*

I truly feel if we were to exchange homes, husband, schedules, calendars, families, ministry, jobs.....there is no way I could do all you do. You know why? Because God gifted you to do what you do, and He gifted me to do what I do. If we swapped, I could not keep your flow as you keep your flow! Our Father created you so precious and unique simply to do what you do. He uniquely knitted your family and set of circumstances, gave you your personality to serve Him.

Given to each of us was a good work created in advance for us to do. So, I say to you *"there is no Glory here for me to take; No pedestal here for me to stand on."* We are **ALL** unique, fearfully and wonderfully made.

Ephesians 2:10
*** God has made us what we are. In Christ Jesus, God made us new people so that we would spend our lives doing the good things he had already planned for us to do.***

A Morning Cup with Honey

10 Of My Fav's

While working with one of my beautiful clients, who was home from college for the Holidays, she was sharing with me a project she was getting started on for school. She had a few questions she had to ask business owners.... One of the questions she asked me I had never thought much about.

She asked, *"What are your top 10 favorite things?"* She then said, *"don't tell me right now just jot them down and text them to me."* I gave her a sideways look and said back to her; *"text them to you?"* Laugh out loud (LOL)....

As I began to jot down my list I realized that most of my favorite things were tied to feelings and didn't have a price tag attached; nor could they be purchased. I found that it is so gratifying to sit and converse with our youth. Not only are we pouring into them, many times we're receiving from them as well.

My 10 included but were not limited to:
- ✓ Laughing hysterically.
- ✓ Big loud family get-togethers.
- ✓ All 3 boys being home together and just watching and listening to them catch up.
- ✓ My honey's car pulling into the garage.

- ✓ Looking out the window at the ground covered in snow.
- ✓ Snuggling on the couch with a nice cup of coffee.
- ✓ A warm bubble bath with a cup of tea
- ✓ A fire in the fireplace.
- ✓ Encouraging surprising and blessing others.
- ✓ A clean house.

What are your 10 favorite things? Jot them down but don't text them LOL…(laugh out loud)

Proverbs 27:9

Perfume and incense make you feel good, and so does good advice from a friend.

A Morning Cup with Honey

You Don't Know

Where is the brotherly and sisterly LOVE?! Many of us do not know what it means to show the genuine love of God to each other. We talk about one another, and we judge each other!

I was speaking with a client the other day. The conversation was centered on her having a severe sinus infection. While going to the grocery store, to pick up a few items and wait for her medication, two ladies decided to laugh at her. She was not dressed fancy; she had a hat on her head and jogging pants. Every time they saw her in the aisle, they would look at each other and snicker to themselves. My client said she looked at them and said to herself "what's so funny?" and proceeded to check out and leave the store. Frankly, my client is very mature and well past caring about what others think of her.

However, what God was revealing to me through her experience was: those two ladies did not know her, but they had already judged her. They were talking about her from her hat down to her jogging pants! As I imagined them talking and snickering at her, I began to understand why things, such as this, traumatize others, who care about how others view them! We all want to be accepted and loved by others! I believe we should treat others the way we desire to be treated. We should have a genuine love for one another; just as Christ instructs us. I am encouraging you to show the love of God, show kindness today.

1 John 4:11
That is how much God loved us, dear friends! So, we also must love each other.

Family Gives Strength

HONEY and I have been in marital covenant for 29 years. We know that complacency blinds us to reality and knowledge sets us free. I am not the authority on marriage; God is. However, I do know this, God loves us unconditionally. That's good news we need to remember often. Struggles in your marriage and your family may be causing great sorrow, fear, or...

Perhaps tension in your marriage threatens to tear it apart. Or maybe pressures from the outside have Disturbed your relationship and made intimacy more of a challenge. You may have made poor or even tragic decisions that have put your marriage in Jeopardy. Whatever your situation whatever challenge you face, God loves you unconditionally, and He wants your marriage, not only to survive but to thrive. Look up, Look to Jesus! Call on Him. Turn to Him now. Invite Him to take control of your marriage. As you pray call the name of your spouse and each member of your family, ask the Lord to intervene and break through some long-standing barriers.

Lady Tonya Dixson

Ecclesiastics 4:9-12
Two people are better than one. When two people work together, they get more work done.
If one person falls, the other person can reach out to help. But those who are alone when they fall have no one to help them.
If two people sleep together, they will be warm. But a person sleeping alone will not be warm.
An enemy might be able to defeat one person, but two people can stand back-to-back to defend each other. And three people are even stronger. They are like a rope that has three parts wrapped together—it is very hard to break.

A Morning Cup with Honey

Quench This Thirsting

I tell you, this world and life have a way of leaving us thirsty. Unfulfilled longings missed opportunities. Regardless of what kind of Life we've LED, eventually we bump up against something that just won't move.

Something we cannot change. Consequences of our own making. Consequences of someone else's making. All of us would like to go back to a day, a weekend or a season of our lives and do things differently. In some cases, we would like to go back in time and urge someone we love to do things differently. But time only moves in one direction.

So, while we are tempted to look back, we can never go back. And it's the looking back that surfaces our thirst, a thirst that seems unquenchable. God's response to the thirsty soul is Grace. God apps for sustaining grace. Grace that leverages the past for a better future. Grace that fills the gaps created by our sin or the sin of others. Grace that allows us to honestly face and carry our pasts but without being controlled by them. Grace that makes the denial unnecessary. You see the grace of God is not limited to an act of God at the time of our Salvation. The grace of God is the life of the savior coursing through the souls of believers to sustain us through those things that will not or cannot change. It is a well of Living Water. It is God's power manifest in our weakness. In this way, the grace of God is a constant reminder of the presence of God. If you have ever gone through a difficult season in your life and felt as if God carried you through it, then you have experienced Grace.

Hebrews 4:16
With Jesus as our high priest, we can feel free to come before God's throne where there is grace. There we receive mercy and kindness to help us when we need it.

A Morning Cup with Honey

Praise to God

First, I just want to thank my heavenly father for revealing Himself to me. I can remember ever so clearly the day that my son sat at the dining room table with me and asked a profound question. "How can God be so powerful yet so personal at the same time." WOW! I was in awe of that, he was so young. I had to figure out how to explain this to him without Honey sitting there with us. It's hard to understand how the Creator God of the universe can also be our personal Savior and call us friends.

No matter how many sermons we hear Bible studies we attend, or how much theology we read, we can't grasp His being both personal Lord and constant companion as well as the Majestic. We tend to stand in awe of that awesome God who made it all and controls it all, but we forget to draw near with the smallest concerns of our day-to-day lives. Or we view Him as close and personal, talking to Him about all that concerns us, but when we slip into thinking, He is so like us that we limit our view of His power and Greatness.

He is both as close as our breath and as expansive as the farthest galaxies. He cares about every detail that concerns us, and yet He controls the movement of the planets and the tides. Part of coming to know Him is learning to live with His mystery, accepting that our view of Him will always be skewed and incomplete. He knows that, too, and He promises that one day we will see Him as He is. Today just praise and THANK HIM! Ask God to open your eyes to more thank Him for His faithfulness to revealing Himself.

Romans 11:33-36

Yes, God's riches are very great! His wisdom and knowledge have no end! No one can explain what God decides. No one can understand his ways.
As the Scriptures say, "Who can know what is on the Lord's mind? Who is able to give him advice?"
"Who has ever given God anything? God owes nothing to anyone." Yes, God made all things. And everything continues through him and for him. To God be the glory forever! Amen.

A Morning Cup with Honey

He Listens

At the end of an extremely long day I must admit that I sometimes found it hard, to concentrate; to sit and listen to my boys when they were little, because of how busy the day had been. Don't get me wrong, I heard them, but I wasn't listening. Those are days and times that I can never get back, but on the upside, I truly learned a valuable lesson from them.

I praise the Lord for listening to me, and I pray that He continues helping me by His Spirit to listen to others. So, few of us are good listeners. Listening takes time, listening is an act of Love. Listening involves eye contact, feedback, and sympathetic responses. Sometimes listening means exercising incredible self-control. It is easier to talk, to tell someone how to fix the problem than it is to sit and listen while they figure it out for themselves.

Listening to a small child or elderly person can be tiresome and irritating when we're in a hurry. Listening is exercising patience. Listening is an act of humility. It's letting someone else have center stage and burying your ego's and need to be seen or in control of the conversation. Listening makes you vulnerable because you never know what news you're about to receive, what secrets you may be asked to keep. God is a true and right listener. He attends to every word, every sigh, every scream, every thought that bubbles up in your mind is heard by God. His ears and His eyes are always turned to His children's voice. Praise Him today for His undivided attention, for constantly listening to the inhale and exhale of your breathing, and beating of your heart, the most secret thought of your mind.

Psalm 66:19

But God did listen to me; he heard my prayer

A Morning Cup with Honey

Obligation to Work

Some people take things so lightly and want to take credit for others hard work. I pray that our Father helps me to continue to be sensitive and forever grateful for the work that He has given me to do, to see it as a gift, His gift to me. I praise God for my Honey and the example that he set in front of our three young boys. We are so very proud of our men. They have grown and have adopted that very same work ethic. We praise God for our grown men. They are very productive members of society.

The world doesn't value work. Many people try to avoid it or get it over with quickly. A- live- for-The Weekend mentality pervades our culture. Some only value certain kinds of work. Work only matters if it pays well or carries Prestige. But work is a gift of God. He values work. He did it for six days in creation. Work is part of our being made in His image. We have a vocational calling. Rather the work is managerial or not is irrelevant. God values them all. He shows no favorites and is not a respecter of persons.

Your diligence and your work, your attention to your work, and your pleasure in your work all matter to

God. They all are opportunities to bring glory to Him and for Him as you flourish where He has placed you.

Jesus work on the cross on our behalf means that God is always pleased with us. He sees us close in Christ's righteousness. God is pleased with our work because he designed it for us, provided it for us, and equipped us to do it. Consider your attitude about work. Thank God for providing pleasure in work.

2 Thessalonians 3:6-9
Brothers and sisters, by the authority of our Lord Jesus Christ we tell you to stay away from any believer who refuses to work. People who refuse to work are not following the teaching that we gave them. You yourselves know that you should live like we do. We were not lazy when we were with you. We never accepted food from anyone without paying for it. We worked and worked so that we would not be a burden to any of you. We worked night and day. We had the right to ask you to help us. But we worked to take care of ourselves so that we would be an example for you to follow.

A Morning Cup with Honey

Do-Over PLEASE!

I think I need a do-over! I LOVE to yell out "He's a God of a second chance every time I fail at something like weight loss. My Honey ever so sweetly reminds me that *"He's a God of another chance and another chance and another chance, you have surpassed a second."* Ok, I get it! Yes, our God is still in the business of do-overs, and the grace of God is sufficient, and it's still readily available. Are you in need of a do-over? Do you need to experience that do-over grace of Him? Our God is in the business of offering you a do-over that can change your life forever!

If you know Jesus as your savior, then you have been redeemed by His blood and forgiven of your sin. To what extent? The verse below says, *"Fully and Freely."* You had a do-over that not only changed your life but exchanged it forever. No matter how deep, how wide, how high, or how far your sin goes, His love and grace go further! Can you Grasp that? He loves you, and if you are in Jesus, you have been given the free gift of Grace! What do you have to do to receive this lavish gift?

Ephesians 2:8 tells us; "For by Grace you have been saved by faith and that not of yourself, it is the gift of God" So, if you are a believer in Christ, Grace is a gift, and it is yours to open and receive!

Ephesians 1:7-8
In Christ, we are made free by his blood sacrifice. We have forgiveness of sins because of God's rich grace. 8 God gave us that gracefully and freely. With full wisdom and understanding.

A Morning Cup with Honey

Pure foolishness

I was "fit to be tied" as Honey, and I sat, having breakfast, listening to the two ladies in the next booth ripping one of their mutual girlfriends to shreds. I couldn't believe the worthless talk that was coming from these two ladies, all their foolishness made me very uncomfortable. The foolish talk includes talking negatively (gossip) or spreading false information (slander) about another person.

Instead of worthless talk, set your mind on building each other up and being a light for others. Not only is this more rewarding, but it also leads to a greater sense of inner peace. So, as you go about your day stop and do an evaluation, ask yourself *"Are a large portion of the words coming from my mouth considered foolish talk?"*

2 Timothy 2:16 (NLT)
Avoid worthless, foolish talk that only leads to more godless behavior.

Meet Lady Tonya Dixson

Lady Tonya Dixson

Lady Tonya Dixson is passionate about three things: The Word of God, Her family and The Souls of men (and Ladies!). All who meet her are drawn to her instantly with her contagious laughter and sweet spirit.
She is married to her best friend - Pastor Kevin Dixson - and serves as her husband's helpmate working Faithfully beside him with dignity and poise.

As a loving mother, she gets the privilege to love on their three blessings – Keith, Kalen, and Keinyi. Additionally, they are blessed to have a beautiful daughter, Jennifer and two grandchildren, Kayleigh and Korey.
She loves that the Lord has let her life be an example of delighting in Him. She watches as He molds her life to make her desires match His.

Lady Tanya holds a degree in medical business administration and is a licensed manicurist. She is also, a successful business owner and entrepreneur for over 23 years.

In February of 2012, she re-launched her Salon naming it after her late mother. Through her business, she has touched the lives of many women by offering Christ and being a great support to them. As such, she founded Sisters In Season (S.I.S) – a women's ministry she shares with other community. She is also the CEO of Designs by Diamonds Daughter; which in cases one-of-a-kind jewelry pieces. They are all designed, handmade, and crafted by Lady Tonya.

While obligations to professional and ministerial commitments are important, Lady Tonya maintains that her primary commitment is to her family. Although she wears many hats, she realizes her first Ministry is to her husband and children.
She firmly believes that no amount of success can compensate for failure at home.

She loves to bring God glory through her roles as Christ -follower, wife, and mother (in that order!). She enjoys singing, ministering to women, creating handcrafting and making jewelry, snuggling on the couch with her honey, cool nights and coffee.

Her greatest desires are to have her marriage bring God glory, see her adult children walk in truth, to lead others to the feet of Jesus, and to lead women into a deeper and intimate relationship with God by encouraging and inspiring them but most importantly through the study of His Word. *A Morning Cup with Honey is* her first book.

Connect with Lady Tonya:

Email: ladytd.sis@gmail.com

Facebook:
https://www.facebook.com/groups/SistersinSeason

www.ingramcontent.com/pod-product-compliance
Lightning Source LLC
Chambersburg PA
CBHW070100100426
42743CB00012B/2608